T0365340

My Friend Middie

a poem about my doggie friend

By Regina Clanton

To order additional copies of this book, contact:
Xlibris
1-888-795-4274
www.Xlibris.com
Orders@Xlibris.com

My Friend Middie

Written by
Regina Clanton

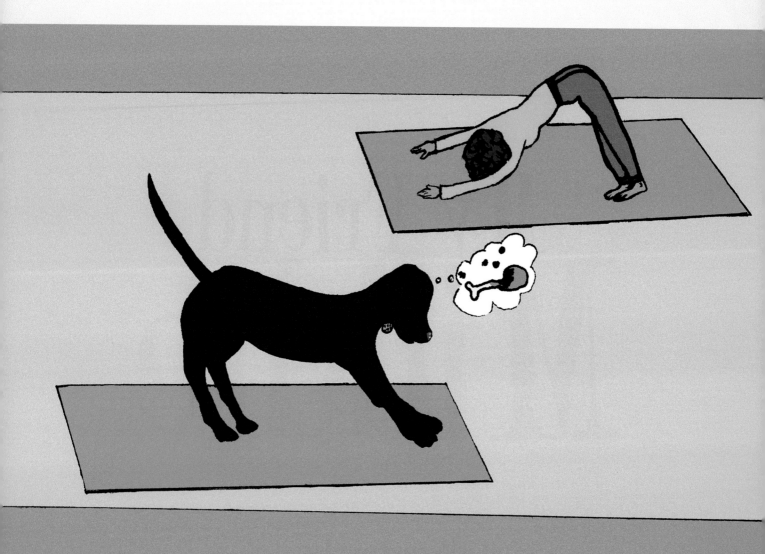

Midnight is my doggie friend.
He's with me all day, to the end.

He is active (as you can see).

His appetite is VORACIOUS !

Check out his running style.
It really is OUTRAGEOUS !

A better companion there could not be.

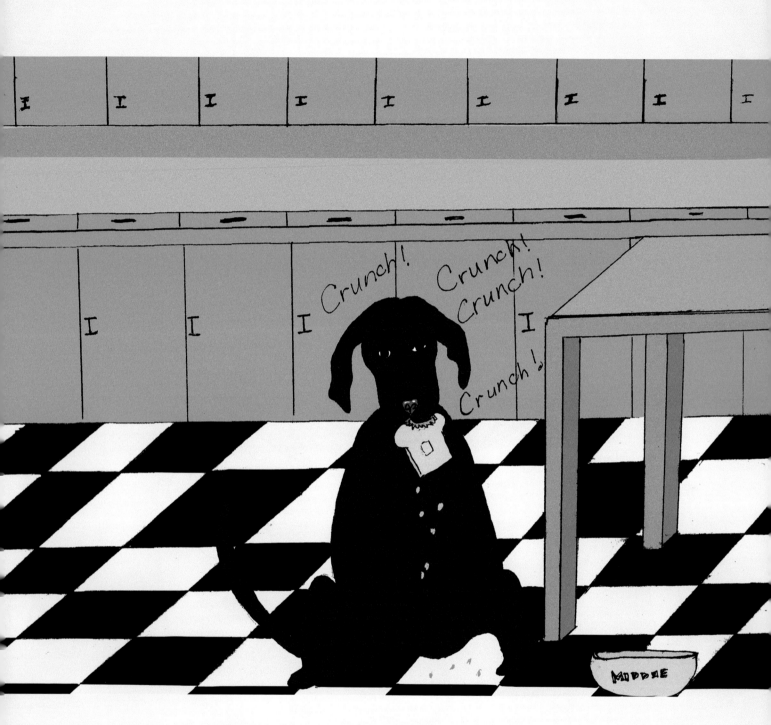

But he eats so much.
He eats constantly.

In the morning he waits patiently.

What's for breakfast ?
What could it be ?

He eats his vittles and then wants mine.
He sets this in motion every day at nine.

My cinnamon toast he thinks is best.
Though he has tasted others as a test.

He would drink my coffee if he could.

Sometimes, I think he's up to no good.

Anything I give is fine you see.
He always gets morsels from me.

Things get better throughout the day. Many scraps are thrown away.

He hangs around and looks forlorn.
Something is bound his way for sure.

Dinnertime is really divine.
The scraps are juicy, oh so fine.

Ohhhhhhhh! That must be why that silly hound, always at my side is found.

I think I know better now.
I'll put him in his place.

Then every day at mealtime, I won't see that woeful face.

Maybe a cat could come
and take his place.

A kitty would not use up
very much space.

But now he's on the outside peering in.

Feeling abandoned by his friend.

For me, I'm sad and eating all alone.

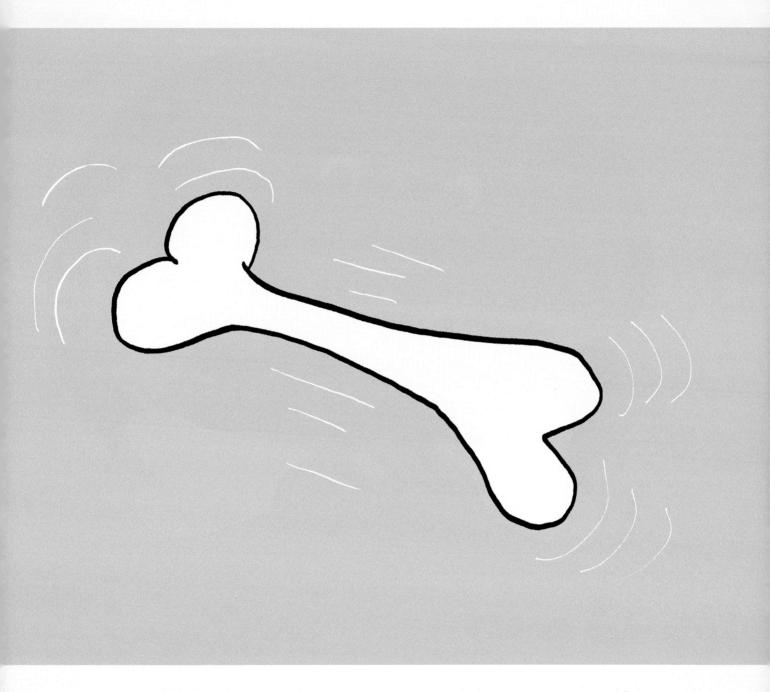

I'll bring him in, cast him a bone!

He sits beside me gnawing merrily.
A happier pooch there could not be.

My doggie friend seems quite content.
Do you see just what I meant?

Printed in the United States
By Bookmasters